STREET RAILWAYS OF EUREKA

By STANLEY T. BORDEN

Eureka Municipal Railway cars in downtown Eureka in 1939.

The Western Railroader
"For the Western Railfan"

VOL. 27, NO. 10   OCTOBER, 1964   ISSUE NO. 297

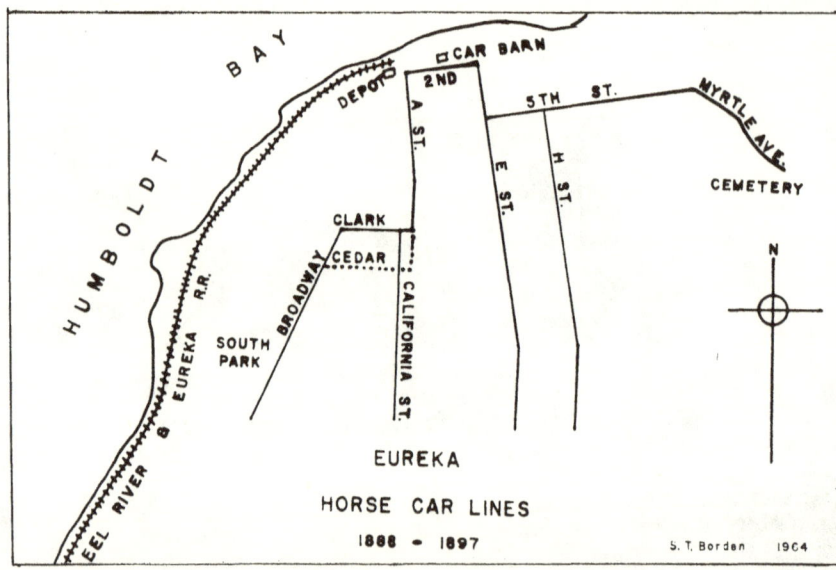

Copyright 1964 by Stanley T. Borden and Francis A. Guido

The Western Railroader
"FOR THE WESTERN RAILFAN"
P.O. Box 668, San Mateo, California
FRANCIS A. GUIDO, Editor-Publisher

Subscriptions: 12 Issues for $1.60
Single Copy 50c

STREET RAILWAYS OF EUREKA

EUREKA STREET RAILROAD

The City of Eureka, California, on June 16, 1887 passed Ordinance No. 111, granting the privilege to construct a street railroad to Richard M. Fernald, Jacob Sowash, E. A. Deming and G. W. B. Yocum. It was to be constructed on 2nd Street from A Street to H Street, H Street to 5th Street to the old County Road (Myrtle Avenue) then to the city limits. Also on C Street from 2nd Street to 3rd Street, 3rd Street to B Street, B Street to Clark Street, Clark Street to California Street and California Street to the city limits. And a line on H Street from 5th Street to the city limits. The work was to commence within one year, the first section to be completed by August 1, 1888 and all lines to be completed within three years. The gauge was not to be more than five feet, fare to be 10¢ or three for 25¢, and the cars to be moved by horses, mules or wire rope.

The Eureka Street Railroad was chartered on October 14, 1887 with Jacob Sowash as president, E. A. Deming as treasurer, B. B. Deming as secretary and Richard Fernald as superintendent, and had an authorized capital stock of $50,000. The local newspaper stated that the company will commence work in the spring and that it will be a pleasant fact to residents in the outlying districts of the city.

The following day it was reported that the company had purchased a lot 30' x 100', 150 feet westerly from the N. E. corner of 2nd and C Streets for $1,000 from M McGarrigan and P. McGarrigan to be used for a car barn and stables for the horses.

A June 23, 1888 newspaper reported that: The street railway people began track laying on 2nd Street near the Eel River & Eureka Railroad depot and that their headquarters building is in the course of erection on 2nd Street and it won't be long ere we may ride about town in true metropolitan fashion. A quantity of iron was looked for on the schooner "Humboldt" but for some reason it did not arrive but there is sufficient quantity on hand to warrant a beginning. In addition to the convenience to the people, this enterprise will be of great value to improvements of streets and is welcomed by the people as the harbinger of a new era of prosperity in Eureka.

On June 30, it was reported that: The track layers find rather tough digging on Second Street, softer ground will be the rule upon the other streets through which the line runs. The schooner "Laura Pike" is coming with the railroad iron and appurtenances for the Second Street line, and upon her arrival rail laying will at once begin. On July 14, it was reported that: The street railway was putting in a turnout on Fifth Street in front of the Court House.

The first line was constructed from the depot along 2nd Street to E Street, E to 5th Street and 5th to Myrtle Avenue. On the evening of August 20th, a trial trip on the passenger streetcar was made over the road from the depot to the terminus at Myrtle Avenue. A crowd of youngsters commenced to gather in the vicinity of 5th and J streets, and followed, yelling, to the terminus. The trip was made without a particle of unpleasantness, the horses working nicely and the car riding very comfortable. After the trial trip, a through trip was made with each car loaded down with children. By next Sunday both cars will be running on schedule time.

On August 25th, it was reported that: The railway seemed to be very fairly patronized and it was thought that the novelty of it attracted passengers rather than the necessity or convenience. The principal amusement of the small fry was in laying rows of pebbles of goodly size on the rails, just to hear the noise when the cars passed over them.

On September 1st: It is said that the daily receipts of the streetcar company have averaged $35 since they started to operate. A nuisance, the street gamins are making the car drivers lives weary by continually jumping off and on the cars while in motion. There is no doubt that some one of them will be killed before long and then perhaps parents will realize that it is easier to prevent, than to remedy.

The next line was built from the car barn on 2nd Street to A Street, along A Street to Cedar Street, Cedar Street to Broadway and Broadway to South Park where the horse facing track was located at Broadway and Wabash. There were passing tracks at 2nd and A Streets and on 5th Street at the Court House. In November the line was extended from 5th Street along Myrtle Avenue to just beyond the gate of the Myrtle Grove Cemetery. Soon after the California and E Street lines were constructed.

There were now three miles of line using 14 pound "T" and 34 pound girder rail, six cars and twenty-five horses. The cost of construction and equipment was $35,000.

In 1890, a line was built on H Street from 5th Street to 16th Street and was put into service on October 11th, bringing the total trackage to 3.5 miles. The fare was 5¢ and 98,620 passengers were carried that year, the gross earning were $5,181 and the expenses were $5,300. At this time Eureka had a population of 4,858.

On November 9, 1892, a petition was presented to the City Council asking permission to extend its lines on E, H, California and Broadway to the city limits (about Trinity Street). The company also wished to abandon that portion of its line on A Street from Clark to Cedar and Cedar to Broadway, and wished to run their line down Clark to Broadway and Broaway to Cedar Street. These extensions increased the mileage to 4.5 miles.

By 1894, R. M. Fernald had become President and General Manager and J. A. Clark was Superintendent.

Mr. Fernald, who was the principal owner, died on March 8, 1897. Apparently the railroad was in poor financial condition due to poor patronization as the road was unable to continue as then organized. The directors passed a resolution the following day to allow the drivers to divide the proceeds if they would feed and tend the horses and keep the road in repair.

The streetcar employees met the evening of March 16th and decided to continue the operation for a few more days until the company could be reorganized providing the people would patronize them enough to pay for running expenses and a bare living.

By March 30th it was apparent that the railway was unable to operate under its present regime as it was tied up with attachments. On the following day the fifteen head of horses were sold by the Deputy Sheriff, bringing from $1.75 to $20.00 apiece, the entire lot brought $97.50. The cars were apparently sold later as most of them ended up in peoples backyards, what was left of the last one was destroyed in 1950.

Roster of Cars

Nos. 1 - 6   Built by Holt, San Francisco
             Purchased in 1888 from the North Beach & Mission Railway, San Francisco.

Humboldt Transit car Number 3 - Lloyd Stine Collection

HUMBOLDT TRANSIT COMPANY

On February 25, 1903, the City Council of Eureka passed Ordinance No. 305 for the construction of a street railroad. The many streets and routes detailed in the ordinance are too many to list and would have pretty well blanketed Eureka with streetcar tracks. Also included was the privilege to carry passengers, mail, express, packages and commodities. The freight was to be carried between 10 p.m. and 6 a.m. but the line was not to carry logs, livestock or explosives. No cars from any steam railroad could be hauled over the line. Daily service was to be provided with not more than one hour interval between cars from 6 a.m. to 9 p.m. The fare was to be 5¢. Work was to commence within six months and two miles of line was to be in operation within 18 months and five miles within 3 years. This franchise was put out for bidders.

On March 2, 1903, George Henderson was awarded the franchise. On April 7th it was reported in the local newspaper that Major J. C. Bull had arrived on the last steamer from San Francisco and stated that every effort was being made by the company to get the construction work started. Because the coast factories were rushed for orders there would be a delay in getting cars, rails, etc. It was intended to put in a 500-horsepower plant to supply the road with power and a temporary power house would be constructed near the Bayside Mill and later power would be brought from the Klamath River where the company intended to install a plant at the cost of about $300,000.

George Henderson stated on June 4th that there would be two miles of road constructed and in operation by September, with ten cars to be used at the outset, power for which would be furnished by the local company. Mr. Henderson, with two experienced engineers in electric road construction,

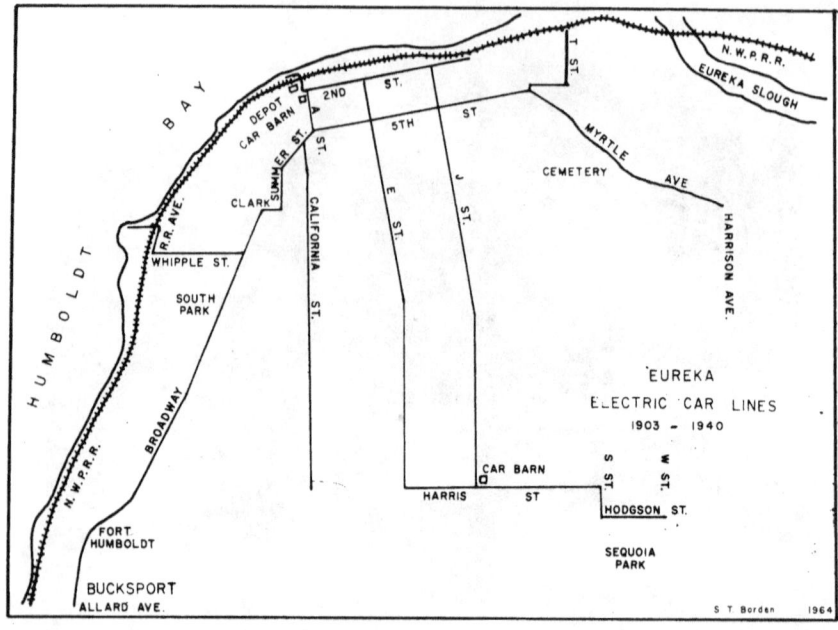

Messrs. Levitt and Fairchild, went over the route and estimated the cost and estimated the cost and construction of the road.

The Humboldt Transit Company was incorporated on July 31, 1903 with an authorized capital stock of $1,000,000 by J. C. Bull, Jr., President; George W. Henderson, Vice President; C. P. Cutten, Secretary; R. W. Bull and J. C. Bull, with the Bank of Eureka as Treasurer. The company was to pay a franchise tax of 3-1/3% to the city and 5-1/4% to the state. On August 14th Henderson transferred the franchise to the company.

With the arrival of the 45 and 60 pound rail, switches and crossings, work progressed rapidly and a car barn was constructed on A Street between 2nd and 3rd Streets. The first six streetcars were purchased second-hand from the San Francisco & San Mateo Electric Railway. The first three arrived on the steam schooner "North Fork" and were landed at the wharf at the foot of C Street. On September 12th the cars were run up from the wharf to the tracks on 2nd and C Streets over temporary track which was constructed on the previous Sunday and taken up after the cars had been brought from the wharf. The cars were California type, open at the ends but closed in the center, painted a lake red with gold trimmings and were capable of carrying as many as 150 people although only 50 could be seated.

The first car to run over the line was No. 1 at 1:30 p.m. in the afternoon of September 12th with Vice President G. W. Henderson and wife; Miss Isobel Henderson, his daughter; Miss Jessie Bull; P. R. Milnes and W. Frank Bull as passengers. The car was operated on 2nd Street, between A and H Streets for two hours to limber it up, and to allow the flanges of its wheels to cut through the bitumen along the tracks. Its operation attracted considerable attention and was followed by a crowd of small boys, up and down the street. That same evening the Vice President took the car up J Street to the end of the line and over the California Street line to Wabash Avenue and reported that everthing was in as good working order as it could possibly be for a new line.

Humboldt Transit line car No. 4 - Lloyd Stine Collection

On the morning of September 15th at 7 a.m. the first cars started running and continued carrying passengers every 15 minutes until 10 p.m. that night. There were a few delays that first day. Twice cars jumped the track at California and Summer Streets but an adjustment of the guard rails soon eliminated this difficulty and 3,000 passengers paid 5¢ apiece for a ride. For many it was a first experience with an electric car, though some had ridden on the horsecar line operated some years prior to this time. Eureka now had a population of 11,111.

When the last car had been put in the car barn on A Street that night, the banquet in honor of the builders of the new line got under way at 10 p.m. at the recently reopened Hotel Vance of E. H. Vance, which had been closed for several years. One hundred fifty prominent Eurekans attended the dinner to hear the ten speakers.

After the first day the schedule was changed to 6:30 a.m. to 11:30 p.m. with cars every ten minutes. The original lines ran as follows: Along 2nd Street from A Street to J Street; along J Street to about 17th Street; along A Street from 2nd Street to 5th Street, Summer Street to Clark Street, Clark Street to Broadway and Broadway to South Park at Wabash Avenue; along California Street from Summer Street to Wabash Avenue; and along 5th Street from A Street to Myrtle Avenue. Despite minor difficulties at the outset, such as derailments and the arrest and court trial of a youngster who put rocks on the track, the electric cars operated successfully.

Within a month work was begun on extending the California Street line from Wabash to Harris Street. Ordinance No. 318 passed on November 13th granted the company the right to build a line on E Street from 2nd Street to Harris Street and soon work was commenced on its construction.

Ordinance No. 344 of June 8, 1904 allowed the company to make a change in the route to Sequoia Park, this line was constructed along Harris

Humboldt Transit car No. 5 - Edna F. Wormell Collection

Street from E Street to S Street, then along S Street to Hodgson Street and along Hodgson to W Street. To help finance the construction of the railway, the company was authorized to issue $500,000 of 30 year bonds to be dated October 1, 1904, carrying 5% interest.

Late in 1904 there was a change of directors and officers, they were: James W. Dawson, President; G. H. Fairchild, Vice President; N. Randall Ellis, Secretary; G. B. Kitch, Superintendent; and A. R. Huntington, with the Humboldt County Bank as Treasurer. There were now 11.3 miles of track in service and an additional three streetcars were purchased at this time.

On January 14, 1905, the street railway was sold to J. E. Green and J. M. O'Brien of San Francisco but the same officers were kept until later in the year when Green became President; O'Brien, Vice President; G. A. Nicholls, Secretary; Milton M. Martin, General Manager; and the Crocker National Bank as Treasurer, with the indication that W. H. Crocker was the real owner.

The City passed Ordinance No. 387 on June 13, 1905 granting the Humboldt Transit additional routes which included the line to the Eureka Foundry. This line was constructed from 5th Street and Myrtle Avenue, east along 5th Street to T Street and then north along T Street to 1st Street.

The company constructed a line west along Whipple Street from Broadway to Railroad Avenue, then north along Railroad Avenue parallel to the steam railroad to about 200 feet north of Cedar Street, then turned west crossing the steam railroad tracks and ran some 400 feet beyond onto a wharf with a 200 foot spur. This wharf was used for unloading new cars and equipment which arrived by steamer. The company also conducted an oil business for many years and this was also handled over the wharf. The

Humboldt Transit car No. 7 - Lyle Wilson Collection

company had constructed their steam electric generating plant here. Cars were also operated on Whipple Street in the mornings and evening for the men working at the Bayside Lumber Company sawmill. For the steam railroad crossing the Humboldt Transit Company and the San Francisco & Northwestern Railway (later Northwestern Pacific Railroad) made an agreement on July 1, 1905 which called for derails on the electric line to be connected with a high two bladed semaphore on the steam line.

Also constructed some time prior to this date was a spur from A and 2nd Streets running north in front of the steam railroad passenger depot, crossing their tracks, then turning west to parallel the steam tracks for a short distance. It is not known actually why this spur was built but it may have been used for the transfer of freight between the electric and steam railways. Also around this time the 2nd Street line was extended from J Street to M Street at the Carson mansion, this line probably served the Dolbeer & Carson Lumber Company employees and other waterfront sawmills. There is no record when these lines were taken up but the depot spur was gone by 1912.

Early in 1906 the company announced that they contemplated extensions to be built that year from Eureka to Arcata and Alliance, 14 miles, and Eureka to Ferndale, 20 miles. Although these lines were not built, the company did acquire six additional cars, one of which was an open cross bench car bought secondhand apparently from Sacramento. This open car was run in good weather mostly between Sequoia Park and South Park horse-racing track at Broadway and Wabash.

In March 1907, the street railway was purchased by George Heazelton of San Francisco who became President; with Burke Corbet as Secretary; Horace R. Hudson, Treasurer; Milton M. Martin, General Manager and Jno.

Humboldt Transit car No. 8 - Second and E Streets
Collection of Lyle Wilson

R. Selby as a director. During this year the Broadway line was extended from Wabash Avenue to Allard Avenue in Bucksport which was a great satisfaction to the men employed at the Holmes Eureka Lumber Company sawmill. This line ran on the side of the road. A line was also constructed on Myrtle Avenue from 5th Street to Harrison Avenue. During the following year George Heazelton announced that he was considering extending the railway to Ferndale and other valley points but like earlier intentions it was never done.

    In the spring of 1910 the company ordered four more streetcars from the W. L. Holman Company of San Francisco which brought the total in service up to nineteen. There were now 13 miles of track. George Heazelton died in July of this year and his widow Mary B. Heazelton became the owner and appointed her brother, William Butterworth as president.

    To cover the cost of the Myrtle Avenue, Broadway extensions and the purchase of the new cars, various notes had been issued and as these were outstanding they were consolidated on December 31, 1911 by at $20,000 note of 7% interest to the First National Bank of Eureka. Sometime around 1912 the line from Myrtle Avenue along 5th and T Streets to 1st Street was abandoned and taken up.

    In 1915 a program of rebuilding the cars was started. The cars were rebuilt with closed ends designed for one man operation. The curved sides were rebuilt straight, air brakes added and four wheel cars were rebuilt as double truck. Some of the older cars were scrapped and many of the cars were renumbered. On August 28, 1915 a new car barn site was purchased at the corner of J and Harris Streets for $4,000. A car barn 240' x 240' with a 70' x 132' shop was constructed and by November 15 all the equipment had been moved to this new location.

Humboldt Transit car No. 12 with crews up the pole to watch horse races at South Park - Joe Moir Collection

From 1912 to 1915 the railway operated at a loss but the oil profits covered it. With the loss of the oil contract the company inaugurated one-man cars to reduce the operating expenses.

In 1918 there were six one-man and three two-man cars in operation but the company was still operating at a loss because of increased costs due to the war time prices so an application was made to the California Railroad Commission for an increase in fare from 5¢ to 6¢. In 1919 there was a strike of the platform men from September 20th to October 4th. The men asked for an increase in pay from 36¢ to 55¢ per hour and an 8 hour day. The company offered 50¢ which the men accepted with no change in hours which were 9-1/2 hours per day.

Reconstruction of the track on Broadway between Clark and Wabash was undertaken in 1920 with 40 and 60 pound "T" rail and new #00 round trolley wire. During the following year 7.7 miles of track was ballasted with Eel River gravel. Early in 1921 the company was in correspondence with the American Car Company investigating the cost of single truck "Birney" streetcars to replace the cars then in service.

Of its authorized stock, the company had issued $500,000 (5,000 shares) which were outstanding. Of the 1904 authorized bond issue, a total of $211,000 had been issued from time to time and $172,000 was still outstanding and no interest had been paid on them in 1920. There were notes due to William Butterworth of $41,000 and to the Peoples Trust & Savings Bank of Moline, Illinois to the amount of $23,716.14. There was a floating indebtedness of about $20,000 which the company failed to pay interest on. The unpaid interest at the end of 1920 amounted to $19,308.90 and the total current liability of the company was $97,038.15.

Humboldt Transit car No. 9 - S. T. Borden Collection

When the Harris Street line was built it had been necessary to build a trestle as the street dipped down into a gully. During October and November of 1915 the City regraded Harris Street and the trestle was removed to lower the track 12'. During the reconstruction the passengers had to walk across to the waiting car beyond.

1915 Schedule

E Street Line	- 1st car leaves Sequoia Park at 6:00 a.m.
	Last car leaves at 12:15 a.m.
California Street Line	- 1st car leaves Harris at 6:00 a.m.
	Last car leaves at 12:45 a.m.
Bucksport Line	- 1st car leaves Bucksport at 6:27-1/2 a.m.
	Last car leaves at 12:42-1/2 a.m.
Myrtle Avenue Line	- 1st car leaves Harrison at 6:20 a.m.
	Last car leaves at 12:20 a.m.
J Street Line	- 1st car leaves Harris at 5:55 a.m.
	Last car leaves at 12:10 a.m.

15 minute headway between cars on all lines.

From 1905 until June 30, 1915 the railway had a lucrative fuel oil business by which it purchased oil under contract from the Union Oil Company at 50¢ per barrel and sold to the public at considerable profit. Even with an increase of cost to 83¢ per barrel on March 1, 1912, the railway still handled 150,000 barrels per year. But with the Northwestern Pacific Railroad's construction completed to the south, other oil companies moved in and the railway lost its contract and ended its fuel oil business when it had to purchase fuel oil on the open market at $1.77 per barrel.

Humboldt Transit car No. 19 - Clark Museum, Eureka

The company operated at a loss from 1912 but from this date to 1915 the company's oil business profit covered this loss but with the loss of the oil contract in 1915 it had been necessary to ask for a fare increase. The fare increase did not cover expenses and the company was still operating at a loss and was unable to continue. The earnings were not sufficient to pay operating expenses, taxes, interest on funded and unfunded debts to say nothing of dividends to stockholders and the setting aside of a depreciation fund. Because of deferred maintenance it would require an expenditure of $37,500 for renewal expenses. To rehabilitate the property with rail renewal and modern one-man cars would require a very considerable outlay of additional capital money which added to the present investment would result in an investment figure so high that the railway would be unable to earn a fair return. The only alternative was to sell to the city or discontinue operations and scrap the railway.

Because the street railway was a necessity to the people of Eureka, the city made plans to take it over. The California Railroad Commission was asked to make a valuation of the property which their engineers set as $100,000 with a scrap value of $40,000 to $50,000. The engineers conclusion that under municipal ownership and operation the railway should earn all of its expenses and would be relieved of taxes and street paving costs.

The city held a special election on June 20, 1921 and the people with a vote of 2514 to 446 authorized an indebtedness of $130,000 to purchase the street railway. On October 15th the Superior Court for Humboldt made an order directing the Humboldt Transit Company property to be sold at a public auction to be held on December 19, 1921. On that date the railway was sold for $111,539.45 to James Walter Scott, who although Vice President of the Humboldt Transit Company, was representing the city. On December 23rd, he in turn sold the railway to the City of Eureka for $10.00.

Humboldt Transit second 13 - Lyle Wilson Collection

Humboldt Transit car No. 16 - Collection of Joe Moir
Other view of car 16 and car 17 of Humboldt Transit
in issue 152 of The Western Railroader.

Humboldt Transit Company

Cars

No.		Trucks	Length	Builder		Became Municipal	
	1	2	28'	O'Brien	scrapped 1919		
	2	2	28'	"	" 1919		
	3	2	28'	"	" 1915		
2nd	3	2	28'	Holman	ex 1st #13	# 3	
	4	2	28'	O'Brien		4	- 01
	5	2	28'	"		02	
	6	2	28'	"	scrapped 1915		
2nd	6	2	28'	Holman	ex 1st #15	6	
	7	1	28'	"		7	
	8	1	28'	"		8	
	9	2	33'	"		9	
	10	2	33'	"		10	
	11	2	33'	"		11	
	12	2	35'	?	open bench car	12	
	13	1	28'	Holman	renumbered 2nd #3		
2nd	13	2	33'	"	ex #19 renumbered 2nd #15		
	14	1	28'	"		14	
	15	1	28'	"	renumbered 2nd #6		
2nd	15	2	33'	"	ex 2nd #13	15	
	16	1	28'	"		16	
	17	1	28'	"		17	
	18	2	33'	"		18	
	19	2	33'	"	renumbered 2nd #13		

Notes:

Nos. 1 - 6 built by O'Brien & Sons in 1892 for the San Francisco & San Mateo Electric Railway series Nos. 16 - 30; purchased in 1903 from the United Railroad of San Francisco.

Nos. 7 - 11, 13 - 19 built by Holman, San Francisco, between 1904 and 1910, and purchased new.

No. 12 open bench car purchased second hand, apparently from Sacramento.

Nos. 1 - 6 had McGuire trucks with two 25 hp WP50 motors and used K-2 controls.

All single truck cars were equipped with Peckham 9-A trucks.

Double truck cars were equipped with St. Louis #43, Peckham or Standard 0-50 trucks with Westinghouse 92-A motors and GE K-10 controls.

No. 4 rebuilt into a line car.

No. 5 rebuilt into a dirt car.

In 1915 the company started rebuilding the cars, single truck cars were made double truck, some of the cars had their curved sides replaced with straight sides, some were made into one-man cars with gates and some were equipped with air brakes.

Eureka Municipal Railway car No. 10 with operator James Poor. This car was rebuilt as car 20. From collection of Lyle Wilson

The Eureka Municipal Railway's "Great Experiement" --the Model A Ford with flanged wheels--from the collection of Lyle Wilson

Downtown transfer point with Eureka Municipal car No. 15 and Ford V-8 bus in 1939.--Stephen D. Maguire collection

EUREKA MUNICIPAL RAILWAY

When the City took over the street railway they received thirteen passenger cars, one line car, one dirt car, one flat car and one two-horse line wagon. The trackage consisted of the: Main Line - from W Street via Hodgson Street, S Street, Harris Street, E Street, 2nd Street, A Street, 7th Street, California Street to Harris Street.
Main Line - from W Street via Hodgson Street, S Street, Harris Street, E Street, 2nd Street, A Street, 7th Street, California Street to Harris Street.
5th Street Line - from Harrison Street via Myrtle Avenue, 5th Street, Summer Street, Clark Street, Broadway to Allart Street.
J Street Line - from E Street via 2nd Street, J Street to Harris Street.
Whipple Street Line - from Broadway via Whipple Street, Railroad Avenue to the wharf.

The Humboldt Transit Company had been purchasing their power from the Western States Gas & Electric Company. Their rotary convertor, transformer and switchboard had been leased from William Butterworth and these were purchased by the City on August 27, 1921 for $5,000.

Although the railway was named the Eureka Municipal Railway, for a number of years the tickets, transfers and conductor's reports were lettered "Eureka Street Railway". The City did considerable rebuilding of the cars and scrapped several. They also renumbered some of the cars by adding a number in front or changing the first number so as to give the impression that there were more cars than there really were and so the numbering was not consecutive.

In July 1928 the track on Whipple Street from Broadway to Railroad Avenue was abandoned and taken up, apparently the track on Railroad Avenue onto the wharf had been removed earlier.

Eureka Municipal Railway work car No. 03 decorated for a parade as N.W.P. No. 1.--Collection of Lloyd Stine.

Eureka Municipal Railway "car burning" at 5th and F Streets on February 24, 1940, with car 18 as the victim. Photo by Lloyd Stine

Eureka Municipal Railway car No. 15 out on the line
July 9, 1938 as photographed by Wilbur C. Whittaker

In the early 1930's the railway tried out a model "A" Ford with flanged wheels to carry passengers but it was not suitable. Towards the end of the 1930's the railway purchased a bus to replace the Broadway streetcar and ran it from 5th and Summer Streets to Bucksport, as the State wanted to improve Broadway and wanted the track removed. About 1938, another bus was purchased and the J Street line was bussed between 2nd and E Streets, and Harris Street.

The railway served Eureka faithfully with good service up until the time that it was abandoned, although there were no new lines built or new cars acquired. It had the occasional derailment, car breakdown, collision with automobiles and going off the end of the track occasionally at the end of the lines with the help of the kids greasing the rails.

The private auto began cutting into the passenger traffic and because the street railway was losing from $10,000 to $20,000 per year, the equipment was in poor condition with the prospect of costly replacement, the City Council decided on September 19, 1939 to junk the railway and replace it with either a city owned or a privately owned bus system.

A special election was called on November 7th with a 4,933 to 2,597 vote to junk the street railway but the proposed expenditure of $50,000 for new buses failed by 87 votes.

The City therefore issued a franchise for a bus system and the Manning Transportation Company was the successful bidder.

Tuesday, February 20, 1940 was the last day of regular streetcar service with the buses taking over the next day. Some runs were made on Saturday, February 24th for a big celebration when car No. 18 was set on

Eureka Municipal Railway Car No. 17 out on the run in 1939

Eureka Municipal Railway car No. 19 on the street in 1939.

fire downtown on 5th Street. The fire got so hot that it scorched some of the buildings and the Fire Department had to put it out. Between May 24th and July 1st, the rails were removed and the car barn was wrecked in December. Thus ended the only electric street railway in the Redwood Empire. The so called improved service with buses soon became very inferior and finally deteriorated to the point where it was abandoned some years ago.

Eureka Municipal Railway

No.	Length	Builder	
3	28'	Holman	renumbered #33
4	28'	O'Brien	" 01
6	28'	Holman	" 16
7	28'	"	" 27
8	28'	"	" 28
9	33'	"	" 19
10	33'	"	" 20
11	33'	"	" 21
12	35'	?	scrapped prior to 1926
14	28'	Holman	" " " 1926
15	33'	"	" 1940
16	28'	"	" prior to 1926
2nd 16	28'	"	ex #6 scrapped 1940
17	28'	"	scrapped 1940
18	33'	"	" "
19	33'	"	ex #9 scrapped 1940
20	33'	"	ex #10 " "
21	33'	"	ex #11 " "
27	28'	"	ex #7 " "
28	28'	"	ex #8 " "
33	28'	"	ex #3 " "

Work Cars

01	28'	O'Brien	line car ex #4	scrapped 1940
02	14'	" ?	flat car trailer	" "
03	28'	O'Brien	dirt car	" "

Notes:
The Eureka Municipal Railway also did considerable rebuilding. The cars which still had curved sides were rebuilt with straight sides; two-man cars rebuilt to one-man; hand braked cars changed to air brakes; the open end sections were closed in with glass windows; and later metal sheathing was applied to the wooden sides.

CREDITS: Author Stanley T. Borden extends thanks to the following for assistance: Lyle Wilson, Lloyd Stine, Steve Renovich, Ruby C. Shanahan, Joe Moir, California Public Utilities Commission and the many who furnished pictures.

Eureka Municipal Railway work car No. 01; former Car No. 4

Eureka Municipal Railway car No. 16 at the carbarn in 1939.

Eureka Municipal Railway car No. 21 sporting the last fancy paint job in late 1939 specially spotted at the car house.

Eureka Municipal Railway car No. 27 also rated the new paint job and special medallion with a redwood tree in late 1939.

Eureka Municipal Railway car No. 28 in the yard in 1939.

Eurkea Municipal Railway car No. 33 in the car yard in 1939.

EUREKA STREETCAR PICTORIAL
Supplement to Issue 297, October, 1964, STREET RAILWAYS OF EUREKA, by Stanley T. Borden

Humboldt Transit laying track on Myrtle Avenue in 1907.
Collection of Lyle Wilson

Humboldt Transit first No. 13 on Myrtle Avenue line.
Collection of Lyle Wilson

Humboldt Transit car Number 10.
Collection of Edna F. Wormell

Humboldt Transit Number 11 at A and Third Streets.
Collection of Lloyd Stine

Humboldt Transit Second Number 13 with a group of crewmen
Collection of Lyle Wilson

Humboldt Transit Number 14 with its crew,
Huey Jones and Lonie Finley
Collection of Lyle Wilson

Humboldt Transit No. 17 in a company photograph used to illustrate the "before" rebuilding.
Collection of Louis Bradas, Junior

Humboldt Transit Number 18 at the A Street carbarn with William Ford, Albert White, Carl Anderson, George Ford, and Ernest Wav.
Collection of Lyle Wilson

Humboldt Transit Car No. 8 as a one-man car at the end of the Broadway line at Bucksport with motorman Frank Frost.   Collection of Lyle Wilson

Humboldt Transit Company shops about 1915 showing first No. 13 being rebuilt and renumbered second No. 3. The 2nd man is Frank Casedy and 5th man is Jack Clark.
Collection of Lyle Wilson

Humboldt Transit shops with a later view of 1st No. 13 being rebuilt as 2nd No. 3...the first One-Man Car.
Collection of Lyle Wilson

Humboldt Transit car No. 16 in a company photograph to illustrate the "after" rebuilding for one-man operation.
Collection of Louis Bradas, Jr.

Municipal Railway Car No. 17 at California and Harris streets in 1940 illustrates the "timeless" character of Eureka prior to World War II. Photograph by Lloyd Stine

Municipal Railway car No. 27 at Clark and Summer Streets in May, 1939, showing unpaved streets and wooden sidewalks in use at that late date. Photograph by Lloyd Stine

Municipal Railway burned car No. 18 and flat car No. 02 being shoved back into the carbarn on February 24 1940.
Photograph by Lloyd Stine

Eureka Municipal bus No. 1 on the J Street run at the carbarn.
Collection of Lyle Wilson.

www.ingramcontent.com/pod-product-compliance
Lightning Source LLC
Chambersburg PA
CBHW031439040426
42444CB00006B/896